EARTH'S ECO-WARRIORS

AND THE FIGHT FOR ECO-FRIENDLY FOOD

WRITTEN BY
SHALINI VALLEPUR

DESIGNED BY
GARETH LIDDINGTON

The Planet Promise

I PROMISE TO:

THINK WHAT I USE AND BUY.

REFUSE WHAT I DON'T NEED.

REDUCE MY WASTE AND CARBON FOOTPRINT.

REUSE THINGS WHEN I CAN.

RECYCLE AS MUCH AS I CAN.

ROT FOOD IN A COMPOST BIN.

REPAIR BROKEN THINGS.

Earth's Eco-Warriors are fighting for eco-friendly food. But what is eco-friendly food and why should we fight for it? Eco-friendly food is food that is sustainable and doesn't damage or harm the environment. Do you know where the food you eat comes from and how it gets to the supermarket? Some foods are grown or transported in a way that can damage the environment. We must rethink what food we buy and think about ways that we can make food eco-friendly.

BookLife PUBLISHING

©2021
BookLife Publishing Ltd.
King's Lynn
Norfolk PE30 4LS

Written by:
Shalini Vallepur

Edited by:
Emilie Dufresne

Designed by:
Gareth Liddington

ISBN: 978-1-83927-148-9

Eco-words that look like this are explained on page 24.

WE ARE EARTH'S ECO-WARRIORS

Are you an Eco-Warrior? Greta, Bailey and Pietro are Earth's Eco-Warriors! Eco-Warriors care about the environment and planet Earth. They made the Planet Promise and are trying to save planet Earth.

GRETA

BAILEY

> Join us, Earth's Eco-Warriors, as we fight for eco-friendly food!

ROCKY

PIETRO

3

Earth's Eco-Warriors were at the supermarket buying tasty fruits for a picnic when they noticed something.

These strawberries were grown in a different country, and look at the plastic packaging it comes in.

Look at the labels on these fruits. Most of these fruits were grown in faraway countries. That means they will have a lot of <u>food miles</u>.

SERVICE DOG

4

What are food miles?

Food miles measure the journey certain foods go on to get to us. The journey starts from where the food is grown and ends where the food is eaten. Food miles also measure how much <u>energy</u> is used during this journey.

5

Some of the food in the supermarket come from faraway places.

The farther a food has to travel, the more _fuel_ and energy is needed to transport it. This can cause a lot of _pollution_ which damages the environment.

Pumpkins from the US

Strawberries from Spain

Lots of people like to be able to buy lots of different foods throughout the whole year.

Avocados from Mexico

Bananas from Brazil

A lot of the food in the supermarket comes from far away because they need certain weather to grow. Luckily, we can still get lots of food from near where we live! Come on Eco-Warriors, let's head to the farmers' market!

Tea from China

Lamb from Australia and New Zealand

SERVICE DOG

7

This farmers' market is so busy! There are lots of <u>local</u> farmers selling the <u>produce</u> that they grow.

The local butcher and baker are here selling their produce too!

Some of the produce here will have fewer food miles because they were grown nearby.

Local farmers and shops also sell seasonal produce. This means the food grows well at that time of year and has been <u>harvested</u> recently.

Earth's Eco-Warriors headed to a nearby pick-your-own farm to pick local strawberries for their picnic.

I love picking local strawberries! It's nice to know that we are eating strawberries that don't have many food miles.

FOOD THAT IS SOLD WITHOUT ANY PACKAGING IS CALLED ZERO-WASTE FOOD.

Let's put the strawberries in our own containers. Strawberries, and other produce in supermarkets, usually come in lots of plastic packaging.

REDUCING WASTE IS A PART OF THE PLANET PROMISE!

By picking our own, we get to enjoy local, seasonal strawberries and reduce our waste. These strawberries are tasty and full of good <u>nutrients</u>.

Plastic packaging

11

Earth's Eco-Warriors enjoyed their freshly picked local strawberries with other fruits and sandwiches at the park. After their big picnic, they started to clean up their waste.

I've put any recyclable packaging in the recycling bin. What waste is left?

Here's some food waste. We can't put banana skins and orange peel in the rubbish bin!

We'll take it to the compost bin! Rotting food is part of the Planet Promise.

ROCKY

13

Are you sure we can put banana skins and orange peel in the compost bin?

Yes. Fruit and vegetable scraps can rot into compost. The compost will be full of nutrients and we can use it to help plants grow.

What else can we put in the compost bin?

SERVICE DOG

Food waste, such as fruit and vegetable scraps, tea bags and coffee grounds can go in the compost bin. We can also put cardboard, paper and black and white newspapers in it too.

Well done, Eco-Warriors! We made barely any waste. Most of our waste can rot or be recycled!

15

Earth's Eco-Warriors headed inside to see what food they had left over from the picnic.

Let's put these leftover sandwiches in the fridge. We can eat them at lunchtime tomorrow.

Food is wasted all over the world. It is important to remember that lots of food can still be eaten the next day or frozen and eaten another time. We should try to only buy the food we need to help reduce our waste and save good food.

SERVICE DOG

Yes. It's also important to eat these foods before they spoil or go out of date. We can take the food that we won't eat in time to a food bank. My mum takes as much as she can to the food bank.

ALWAYS CHECK WITH AN ADULT BEFORE YOU EAT LEFTOVERS.

Pietro, let's ask your dads if we could take some food to the food bank. This will mean that nothing will go to waste!

Food banks accept all types of food, but let's take some food that can last for a long time, such as dried pasta and cans of soup.

Beans

Por

Food banks help to stop food from going to waste. Sometimes we buy more food than we need. We may not need all the food, but somebody else might!

Thank you for bringing all of this lovely food.
So much food gets thrown away everyday while many people around the world don't have enough to eat.
Exactly. We can take these cans and give them to people who may be in need of food.
Porridge
DONAT

We've done a lot, but the fight for eco-friendly food isn't over yet! We need to keep fighting for eco-friendly food to help the environment and the planet.

We've had such a busy day fighting for eco-friendly food. We've picked our own, made compost and taken things to the food bank.

21

WHAT'S IN SEASON?

Let's make a food calendar! You can use the food calendar to keep track of what foods are in season. This will help to make your food miles lower and reduce pollution in the environment!

THINGS YOU WILL NEED

Large piece of card

Ruler

Coloured pens and pencils

ASK AN ADULT TO HELP YOU FIND OUT WHEN DIFFERENT FOODS ARE IN SEASON NEAR YOU.

22

Spring	Summer
Autumn	Winter

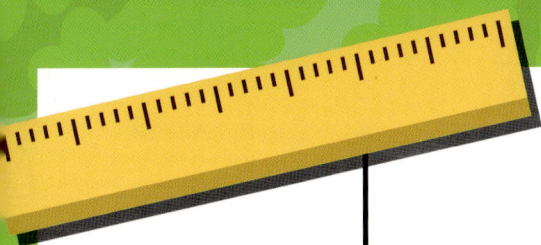

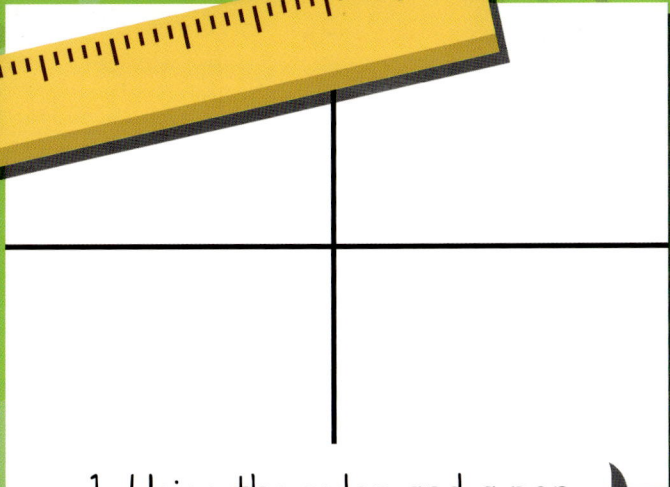

1. Using the ruler and a pen, draw lines on the card to make four sections.

2. Write each of the seasons in each section.

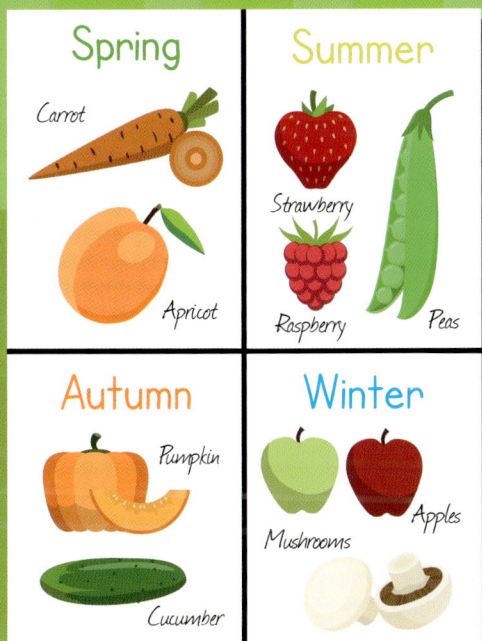

Spring	Summer
Carrot	Strawberry
Apricot	Raspberry	Peas
Autumn	Winter
Pumpkin	Apples
Cucumber	Mushrooms

3. Ask an adult to help you find out what grows locally in each season where you live.

4. Draw your favourite fruits and vegetables in the seasons they grow in.

23

ECO-WORDS

compost bin	a special bin where garden waste and some food scraps such as vegetable peel turn into soil
energy	a type of power, such as light or heat, that can be used to do something
environment	the natural world
food miles	a measurement that tracks how much energy is used in transporting food
fuel	something that can be used to make energy or to power something
harvested	when fully grown crops have been picked
local	found, grown or made in a place that is nearby
nutrients	natural things that plants and animals need in order to grow and stay healthy
pollution	harmful or poisonous things being added to an environment
produce	plants that have been grown to be eaten such as vegetables
rot	when something breaks down and decays
sustainable	to be done in a way that doesn't harm the environment or use up Earth's natural resources
transported	to have carried something from one place to another

INDEX

PHOTO CREDITS